ROYAL GENERATION

By Timothy Torres

⁹ But you are a chosen generation, a royal priesthood, a holy nation, His own special people, that you may proclaim the praises of Him who called you out of darkness into His marvelous light;

¹⁰ who once were not a people but are now the people of God, who had not obtained mercy but now have obtained mercy. (1 Peter 2:9-10 NKJV)

Table of Contents

Challenge from the Writer

This book is for every believer, and possibly those who aren't yet believers, but whose hearts are searching for His Truth. It's one small tool to encourage and ground them into seeing their new identity and love relationship with Christ — a royal glimpse of identity through the Gospel — creating a picture of love and Royalty. 1 Peter 2:9 is the heart cry of a King to be close to His children.

Embrace the challenge in this book— to read this book in one uninterrupted sitting. If you want to be thirsty for God or are thirsty for the heart of the Father, immerse your heart in this book. As we gaze at an object of beauty like the sunset, sunrise, a starry night, or painting; we never look at it in several portions. We view it all at once to try and catch all the majesty of the creation. If you're busy today I encourage you to find the available time with no agenda. Read this book in one sitting and fall more in love with Jesus.

Preface

⁷ Therefore, to you who believe, He is precious; but to those who are disobedient, "The stone which the builders rejected Has become the chief cornerstone,", (1 Peter 2:7 NKVJ)

Jesus loves you so much!

In this book you will see how He laid His life down for you in ways no man ever could. You will see how God loves you and gave His Son so you may become royalty, our *royal generation*. You will see the love behind the cross and it will lead you to your identity in Christ Jesus. But most importantly, I hope, by reading it, you will not only see a picture of your identity as *royalty*. But, a picture of a God that loves you so much He gave Himself so He may have a relationship with you. Out of that deep love that one could only attempt to comprehend, flow our roots in royalty — that royalty is a byproduct of His love relationship with us.

But we should find contentment in our relationship with Jesus alone...

Introduction

⁹ But you are a chosen generation, a royal priesthood, a holy nation, His own special people, that you may proclaim the praises of Him who called you out of darkness into His marvelous light;

¹⁰ who once were not a people but are now the people of God, who had not obtained mercy but now have obtained mercy. (1 Peter 2:9-10 NKJV)

Jesus is a king in God's government and God's government is a monarchy. Meaning it has a king and a kingdom and we are part of that kingdom! Praise Jesus!!! Based on 1 Peter 2:9, we see we are a *royal* and a *chosen generation*. Wow! God chose us!

A *royal generation* is our new identity according to verse 10! It is important to know our identity, so in life as we face people, negative thoughts, and situations that need faith we will be equipped with who we are in Christ's kingdom and can walk it out. Most of the time, people don't care how much you know until they know how much you care. Romans 5:8 shows us God definitely had a solution for that! It says, "He demonstrates His love for us while we are still sinners!" That means He knew we have a choice and still may not even come to Him, but He did it anyway.

In each chapter of the book you will see how He performs love in action to establish your identity.

Sometimes others would attempt to kill the king to take reign over his kingdom. Jesus paints a picture for us in the garden of Gethsemane. He knows the painful cost of the cross and asks God, "If it be your will, take this cup from me." Not a literal cup but the crucifixion for our sins. In ancient Kingdoms the King would employ a servant to be his cup bearer. A cup bearer would drink from the cup before the king to ensure no poison would ever reach the king's lips and kill him. Jesus knew the pain and torture He was facing, He is our King, and He still drank the deadly poison for us.

Relationship

*¹³ Greater love has no one than this,
than to lay down one's life for his
friends. (John 15:13N KJV)*

Jesus laid His life down for us and there is no greater love than that!

John 3:16 tells us God loved us so much that He sent His Son, Jesus, to come take our place and die. Now, because of His sacrifice, all who believe in Jesus are now God's children! We are princes and princesses. Now we are the children of a real God! Just think about that...a real and beyond giant God. The Creator of everything did that knowing we may reject Him, just so you could have a choice — a choice to be part of His divine kingdom. We now have the opportunity to worship and live for an amazing God.

Before Jesus died on the cross we were subject to the old covenant (promise). Under that covenant, only once a year one priest would go before God's presence in the Holy of Holies, which was God's residence on earth (Hebrews 4:7). Now, through Jesus and the new covenant, we are all granted the privilege to go directly before God's presence to worship, pray, repent, or fellowship (1 Peter 2:9).

We are now spiritually in Christ seated in Heaven; our citizenship is in Heaven (Philippians 3:20/ Ephesians 2:1). Without Jesus, we could never go before God...imagine that! Talk about an incomplete relationship. Could you imagine marrying the love of your life and then never seeing them again, and then only living off the love letters you wrote them? (The Bible is His love letter to us.) Why would we do that to God? He wants so desperately to spend time with us. He loves us more than anyone else! But, He cannot be just a priority in our daily checklist, where we just wake up to read one sentence from His love letter and then ask for a blessing. We must know in our hearts that spending time with God is a priority.

We have to spend time with Him like we would any other relationship. We have to learn to acknowledge His presence just like we are breathing; all the time. In Him we live and move and have our being (Acts 17:28). We should be so in love with Him that we crave spending time with Him and it doesn't become just another "great idea" lost in our busy earthly schedules. God doesn't want us to cry out for Him in the last days, "Lord, Lord" and His reply be, "Away from me, I never knew you!" Our relationship with God is meant to be monogamous (having only one God). He should be our only God and if there is anything or anyone that we make more important than Him, then we are making it our god.

Get in the Kings/Fathers presence and don't stop falling in love.

Image

*[19] Or do you not know that your body
is the temple of the Holy Spirit who is
in you, whom you have from God, and
you are not your own?
(1 Corinthians 6:19 NKJV)*

Jesus is the perfect image. We are God's sons and daughters; we are His children. We should look like Him and we do. An earthly royal image is all about outward appearance. A heavenly royal image in God's Kingdom is much more than an outward appearance but our heart and eternal image. Being like Jesus is exactly that; "being" like Jesus. Not necessarily doing things to be like Him; but becoming like Him at heart. Not just outward actions fueled by religion and obligation. Of course, we should obey the Word of God and do the things He instructed to us. The Bible tells us to clothe ourselves in love (Colossians 3:14). But if it's just the outward clothing of our physical life and actions, is it really clothing our heart at all, our eternal image (Matthew 23:27)? It then becomes God "like" clothing with a God like appearance, but not doing the real thing. Christianity is an internal experience exploding to the outside of our lives and touching the lives of the people around us. If you're doing it out of fulfilling a religious carnal checklist, then you should seek to fall in love with Jesus more. Love should always be our motivation (1 Corinthians 13:1-13).

I encourage you to get alone and spend time with God and just because you don't feel Him doesn't mean He isn't there. Tell him how much you love Him and want to love Him more. The goodness of God will lead us to repentance (changing of the mind), the Holy Spirit will bring you a new conviction to your heart with His love. So in obeying the Word, you will also have a spiritual experience. Our spirits last forever, but our physical body and life do not. Jesus wasn't telling us, just what to do but, also who we should be. Sometimes nonbelievers see Christianity as a lifestyle of going to church and acting a certain way rather than *a relationship of love*. This leads them to choose not to be a part of the Christian lifestyle. We have to continue to spend time with God to abide in Him (John 15:5-9). Leaving our hearts open so Christ may live through us and so we are not doing all the work (Galatians 2:20). It's our job to touch the hearts of people; not change them. Sometimes people's challenges are simply just people's challenges and not always their secret sin. It's a privilege to be a conduit for the Holy Spirit, but not do all the work with a Holy Spirit like work ethic. The Old Testament was about being obedient to the law, the New Testament is about Christ living through us being obedient to Gods will, because He only does the will of the Father.

This is why people get burnt out and quit God or church— because they are trying to clothe themselves in God independently without God by just obeying rules. You're either obeying the Word because your heart's desire is to please God, or you're enduringly grudgingly obeying the Word because you feel like you have too, in order to appear righteous or religious, or you're people pleasing. But, when your heart sincerely desires to please Him, you have had true repentance and heart change. How we appear is not the defining factor of our image. **The way Jesus was a manifestation of God** (Colossians 1:15)**, is the way we should be a manifestation of Christ & walk in love** (Ephesians 5:2).

Put on love daily, to show the love of God to the people He created. He wants relationship with His creation. We are the tools He uses to show His love. Carnal self-image and self-esteem should not be the fuel for our life, but Christ living through us. We must focus on Christ not ourselves. There is a difference between living right and living for God, one is in vain. Suicide everywhere is unfortunately rampant taking people's lives. People are judging how they look or how their lives are and are not looking at Christ or what He did for us. All media marketing is to make money, but people believe the marketing is how they are supposed to look. It's a fallacy especially when half the models don't really look the same in person as they do on the covers of magazines. Our bodies are the temples of the Holy Spirit so we should nurture our bodies but not worship them (1 Corinthians 6:19).

How we look outwardly is not even relevant to God because God states He judges the hearts (1 Samuel 16:7). So who are we to judge the outward appearance of lives, including our own if God doesn't even judge it Himself? Some people are born looking different or with deformities. I know we try to figure it out and ask "Why God?" but the thing is to be like God and align our thoughts with His. So when we look at ourselves or others we should look through the eyes of God (1 Corinthians 2:16) and by their heart not outward insignificant appearance (Matthew 7:24). Appearance will one day return back to the dust of the earth anyway (Ecclesiastes 12:7). Yes the Bible does teach our spirit is righteous before God. People may feel far from God because they analyze their imperfections and see a gap. But God is not far from them. He is omnipresent and His love is greater than a gap. Just acknowledge Him. We will go to heaven when we are saved and no longer having eternal condemnation (Romans 5:9). But it is our position to clothe the heart with the right motive — *for we are God's royal children.*

Authority

¹⁵ He is the image of the invisible God, the firstborn over all creation.

¹⁶ For by Him all things were created that are in heaven and that are on earth, visible and invisible, whether thrones or dominions or principalities or powers. All things were created through Him and for Him. (Colossians 1:15-16 NKJV)

Jesus is the "ultimate" authority. He is the supreme authority over all creation (Colossians 1:1516/ Colossians 2:10). The greatest act of love we could do with anything God gives us is to give it back, so He can use it as He pleases. All authority was given to Jesus by God, and God brought us out of the dominion of darkness into light. Jesus gave us authority over the darkness (Matthew 10:1). So we are not just out of the darkness but have authority over it (Colossians 1:13). He allows us to have partial authority over our life; that we may be the author of our future. We need to sync our will with His; so then He can live through us without us being distracted by our earthly view of how life should be (Galatians 2:20). When we give Him the pen back, He may fulfill the thoughts and plans He has for our lives (Jeremiah 29:11).

Jesus walked with authority everywhere He went when He and saw darkness, He would deliver light with the authority of God. As we also walk into any dark situation we should do as Jesus did and exercise our authority to deliver light over all evil, sickness, and creation.

Authority is like a license, but not the materialistic, earthly badge that can be removed. God's authority is not like earthly authority that can be disobeyed. When it is delivered it creates a whole new state of existence for the recipient. **God used authority over chaos/darkness and said let there be light and there was light. Darkness didn't sit back and say "Hmmm...Do I really want to do this?"** No! It immediately reflected what was authorized and became light! (Genesis 1:3) Praise God!

On Earth a king may give you a ring, robe, or a crown to represent his authority, but in God's supernatural kingdom, He gives His name and Himself. The King literally comes to live in you. Ha-ha! That's my favorite part! We don't need a badge, He lives in us! If anything is freely active, it is because God allows it and in our lives and we allow it; we must exercise our authority and bring it into subjection to God's kingdom.

I encourage you to walk this earth with the authority that has been given to you. Also exercise the authority of the name of Jesus that every knee will bow.

- Walk in authority over creation like when Jesus cursed the tree (Mark 11:12-25)

- Walk in authority casting out demons in the name of Jesus (Matthew 10:1/ Luke 10:17, Philippians 2:9-11)
- Walk in authority healing the sick (Matthew 10:8/ Matthew 10:1)
- Walk in authority and speak against the evil powers and principalities that rule that atmosphere, verbalize to the situation and the atmosphere telling them to submit to the name of Jesus.

When I truly began to see authority working in my life is when I began to pray for people's healings. I stopped taking my hands off them and having that 50/50 feeling of "I hope God will heal them" or gritting my teeth trying to force my mind to believe. But just believing God is a Big God and He will (John 6:29). Take authority! The King lives in you!

Power

[37] For with God nothing will be impossible. (Luke 1:37 NKJV)

Jesus is the word in the flesh. All of God's word is powerful! (Luke 1:37) **If the word says out of the abundance of the heart the mouth speaks** (Luke 6:45) **then the word of God is a glimpse of our Fathers heart!** It is a written and spoken extension of Himself. The word of God is not just a message but a message full of the living spoken words of God that touch and transform (Hebrews 4:12). We are called to be messengers in the kingdom, like a paint brush stroking the world with the heart of God; the powerful word of God bringing the creation of His kingdom back to its original state. So many times people try to interpret the "tone of God" through the Word by stories like Jesus in the temple driving out sin or Nathan telling David "you are the man!" But just because in the verse it has an exclamation point doesn't mean Nathan was screaming angrily; he could have been hugging at the time for all we know. Jesus was in the temple transforming it; cleansing it of sin just like the Holy Spirit cleanses us as temples. God didn't create you to always be angry at you, but to love you. Remember He gave His Son for you!

He may get angry at the sin in our lives but the goodness of God brings us to repentance. We should share the Gospel of His goodness with ourselves and others because Isaiah 54:9 promises that He would be angry with us no more. The word of God is not always angry with us, but it is always alive, powerful, and it can transform everything (Hebrews 4:12). It's important to know what the word of God is and what it is not. Jesus came to save us not destroy us (Luke 9:56 AMP).

Our tongues also have power (Proverbs 18:21). This means we also have the power to give life or destroy it. That is why we must speak the Word of God for our life, for the people around us, and for the world. We must sync our words with God's word. When we curse the creation with our words, we are insulting the loving Creator. James 3:9-10 reminds us that **our words are powerful but using the word of God in our mouth is even more powerful!**

Find the heart of God in any situation and speak over it and it will transform into how God's heart intended it to be. The power of the Holy Spirit also transforms. The uniqueness between the power of God's Word, the power of our tongue, and the power of the Holy Spirit is the Word of God has to be delivered. The tongue gets to choose to bless or to curse, and you have power when Holy Spirit's presence comes upon you (Acts 1:8). The Holy Spirit's presence and power becomes a part of you. That power then has to be released. For example, when the woman with the issue of blood received power from Jesus and was healed. Another example was when Peter's shadow healed the people. The Holy Spirit is not limited to us but does use us to make connections with people to receive the loving presence and power. I like to use the example of a plasma ball —nothing without God, powerful with Him, and just pretty if we only sit and do nothing with the power. Use your prayer language of tongues that you were given or soon will be given, to continue to charge your faith (Jude 1:20 / Romans 8:26).

These are all the life giving powers you have as a royal child of God. Use them! **You are not just a powerless church member but a powerful son and daughter in the Kingdom of God!**

When I was 18 I really began to seek God to be baptized in the Holy Spirit. I wanted all that God had for me. I desired that sacred prayer language (Romans 8:26), so I attended a church service specified for people to be baptized in the Holy Spirit. But after the meeting it seemed everyone had been baptized except me. I was very heart broken and upset at God. The people then funneled into a reserved eating area. Being around the Pastor, he could tell I was very upset. So he asked if I would like the key to our prayer room, I said, "Yes." I just knelt down on my knees with my hands on an old church pew and began to worship God; asking Him to baptize me and give me a prayer language. Before I knew it, the sweet presence of Holy Spirit overtook me. I then began to cry and repent of every little sin I could remember back to when I was 4 years old, to even stealing bubble gum in a store. Another language began to just flow from my mouth. In that moment I began to realize how loving He was. His love felt so embracing and tangible.

Protection

*[11] "I am the good shepherd.
The good shepherd gives His life for
the sheep (John 10:11 NKJV)*

Jesus laid down His life for us and still cares about the safety of your daily lives. (John 10:11) Jesus bulldozed grace into our lives to protect our eternal being; when He sacrificed His life by being nailed to the cross (John 1:17). To even try to comprehend the amount of protection we presently have, we need a vastness of grace in our understanding — the Holy Spirit.

Satan is the God of this world like the word of God clearly states he is (2 Corinthians 4:4). **Grace is God giving Himself when we are not enough — He can when we can't.** Satan and his evil buddies (Ephesians 6:12) are roaming this world to destroy the lives of people (Job 1:7/ 1 Peter 5:8 / John 10:10). But even though he is out to destroy our lives like a furious mercenary; you have made it this far and you're reading this book right now! Imagine the sky with all its stars, or the ocean with all its waves, we look at it but cannot fully grasp it because our eyes are too small! (Psalm 40:5) **Now! Imagine all the protection in your life, you look at it but cannot fully grasp it because your eyes are too small.**

Our human understanding cannot comprehend all of God's efforts for us in the spirit. Jesus died for us because He loves us. And fully comprehending God's love for us is the same way — it's too big. But trying to understand how much He loves us will help us understand how much His heart desires to protect us. Just like Satan is present in the spiritual realm, so is God. Minor or fatal matters of life, God and His angels are present with us (Hebrews 13:5/ Psalm 91:11). Believing this is very important! Acknowledge God's presences and listen for His voice in you (Isaiah 41:10).

I know at times we become very comfortable in our successes but we are still striving for perfection in the things we do achieve. We weren't alone. God was giving grace (2 Corinthians 9:8). But often when something does go wrong, people begin to blame God. What is most important is we're passionately pursuing God. That is the main agenda of every agenda. But God's desire is for us to have an abundant life (John 10:10). In those situations, Satan and your carnal mind may try to put the blame on God. But we have to not use our own understanding but meditate on God's love for us and trust Him (Proverbs 3:5-6). Just like Satan snuck in to turn Adam and Eve against God, he wants you and I to turn against God.

But, truly all the devil does in attempting to destroy lives is give God an opportunity to bless His people. Even in the toughest situations we have to be able to look things in the face, know God's presence is with us, and say, "I trust you Father." (Proverbs 3:5-6). God states repeatedly in the Bible that He is with us and protecting us. God's protection for His children in the kingdom is more than just words on a page, because, once again, the Father –the King – is with you (Hebrews 13:5).

The key is not blaming Him in the negative but believing He and His angels are with you protecting you. Thank Him for the vastness of protection on your life that you cannot see. Listen to His voice to do your part. God is aggressive and ferocious about protecting us. Thank Him in the little moments. When I stubbed my toe or when my parents passed away, 11 months apart, I could have used my human thinking and resented God, but I know I won't understand it all. But, what I do know is His love is greater than any misunderstanding!

Jesus is the precious, valuable of all valuables (John14:6). Jesus is an anomaly! He is the only portion of our provision that gave Himself that we would receive all the fullness of the kingdom of Our Father. Without Him giving of Himself we would be lost and living a gamble. Like the non-believer, the surface of our life may seem fine but their eternal life will be in hell without the presence of God (Psalm 73:17). We need Jesus to obtain eternal life with the Father and to live our daily Christian life on Earth. When we abide in God and sync our wills with His, we receive the provision we need for our soul, for our physical body, and for our life. But what's most important is that we are in communion with God continually, because that is how we walk out our lives, situations, and what matters in eternity. **Meaning, the depth that your soul is impacted by**

the Holy Spirit dictates the way we live and the degree of our surrender (Galatians 5:22-23).

The fruit of the Spirit (love, peace, joy, etc.) is how we internally keep an atmosphere of heaven in us. I've lived well and I've lived poor eating old food or not eating at all. It made me see that everything we think we need is not really a need at all. It helped me realize what true needs really are. I've seen both sides and having a bank account full of stagnant money is really not that important. Don't always view yourself in the desert; it's just an opportunity for God to be glorified. It may make us feel comfortable or secure on earth, but really your security in this eternal life is with His presence. Keeping trust in mind will alleviate some of the fears associated with lack or what we think lack is with or without, God is the true provision. He is our strength (Philippians 4:12-13) and we can find satisfaction in Him alone (Philippians 3:8). Although we do have a full inheritance from God, we shouldn't be misled by it as the center of our life. God is miraculous and doesn't need to always fill a need with money to meet a need. His grace and mercy may just fill the need and you may receive your provision or it may even be alleviated.

God is a God of His order and just because it doesn't go the way we plan; doesn't mean it's not coming to fruition in our life. **The structures of man are not the same as God's order.** God sometimes may even provide a creative miracle. In Bible School, I remember my best friend and I loaded up and left to drive to our church about 48 minutes away.

We realized we only had a quarter tank of gas to drive about 2 hours there and back. We both shrugged our shoulders and laughed not having any other options. We laughed and spoke the name of Jesus over the car to make it there and back to our dorm. Well on our way back to the dorm after church about 5 minutes away; we realized we had forgot all about the fuel issue. We looked at the tank and it was still at a quarter tank! This time we laughed in AMAZEMENT and praised God!

When we focus on the greatness of God, it enables us to see how much bigger He is than our need. We have to stay in love with Jesus. Remember He is the vine that produces in our life. There are so many spiritual principles that God has provided for us. In church, it's common to hear sayings like, "A seed will meet the need (Genesis 8:22/ Luke 6:38)" or "Speak it into existence (Proverbs 18:21/ Romans 4:17)" and "Believe you receive (Matthew 21:22)." These spiritual principles are nothing within themselves. They are a tool God has given us to walk in faith toward Him. God has to be the main focus and not removing God from the equation and standing on the principle alone. **Depending on spiritual principles alone is missing out on the intimacy with Jesus** (John 5:39).

When you seek God the fruit comes (Matthew 6:35). Reducing an understanding of Him to just formulas instead of believing God himself will provide. God's words of love are more than just formulas (John 5:39). God loves us so much. He has a best for us, and He is the best way to obtain it. A common way of thinking regarding the fullness of

God's inheritance for our life is to settle for nothing less than God's best. Steak and ground beef are not entirely different; neither is generic or name brand. The image value that something has doesn't make it God's best. Valuing the importance of receiving our kingdom inheritance is significant, but placing the value of our life in the material value of the inheritance is not God's best. Just because you think you missed out on the most expensive item, of what you think is God's best, don't think you missed out on God. There is always something more expensive. Culture influences how people view the value of blessing. It influences you if it's God's best or not, always focusing on the next best when there is always something bigger will keep us on a never ending journey of wanting.

I'd hate to spend my life always believing for something and never having an intimate relationship with God. In heaven we won't even have monetary value or currency that I know of. But, we will actually walk on gold, which is a form of currency we have on Earth. God's best may not be what we think it is so we must stay in His will. He can bless even more than King Solomon if He wants to, but His will and direction will get us there. The materialization of our provision flows out of our intimacy with Jesus. Not from religious methods for gaining provision taking the place of acquiring provision through the Holy Spirit and His direction. Abiding in God isn't just living by His Word, but also by walking in His presence (Matthew 6:35). Being in God's presence helps to clarify needs and wants in our life through God's Word and intimacy with Him. We will know

His will and what to ask for when we extend our faith asking in the name of Jesus (John 15:7).

We already own our inheritance but our faith and intimacy with God cause it to materialize in our life. Recognize the times you've seen God extend His love to you in your life. Recalling these times will give you faith. We are hidden in Christ and we have our identity in Him (Colossians 3:3). Through our identity in Him we receive. He is the gatekeeper and is always ready to give. We are sons and daughters of the King. He is the author and creator of all things, and He wants to bless you more than you want to be blessed (Luke 12:32). **Jesus alone in himself is enough; the other blessings are just a bonus.**

Vocation

(Calling–Service–Purpose–Holy Career–Privilege)

[18] Now all things are of God, who has reconciled us to Himself through Jesus Christ, and has given us the ministry of reconciliation,
(2 Corinthians 5:18 NKJV)

Jesus is the host message of every message. He restored us to the Father (2 Corinthians 5:18). We also have been given the ministry of reconciliation, which means to restore people's relationship with the Father. This is our service in His kingdom (2 Corinthians 5:20). **The salvation message isn't the only message that should lead you to Jesus; every message should lead you to Jesus,** because Jesus enables us to offer ourselves in communion to God (1 Peter 2:5). Through Jesus we are reconciled to the Father. Not just once at salvation but continually restoring our intimacy to the Father. God wants us to be like Him, but even more He wants us to walk with Him every day on Earth like people did in Eden — continually meeting and developing the beauty of Earth (Genesis 1:2/Psalm 16:9/Psalm 89:15). The core/heart of reconciliation is freely having a constant personal relationship with His children.

The thought of walking next to God humbles me so much — that He would want to be close to me! It reminds me that I am like Elijah — just a man (Jeremiah 5:17). I never want to think I can fully see and comprehend the vastness of God's life or the universe. **The moment I think I can fully see, then I am blind** (John 9:39). I could never do anything out of my own goodness.

It's a privilege to be an ambassador of love in the kingdom. God works through us like He spoke through Balaam's donkey in Numbers 2:28. I'm no better than the guys next to me but equal, we all have sin because we are not God, and are lost without God and need His grace. But when I do begin to release the love of God into people's lives I do it with God no matter the person.

Always keep your eyes on Jesus even when you're looking at someone else. He is the ultimate filter and will filter anything out that is not of love. Once I had an indifference towards someone, but God spiritually massaged it in my heart to see them the way He saw them (2 Corinthians 5:16). Through His eyes, I could see them with compassion. They needed God's love like all of us do. I had to choose to let that love come through me. Sometimes that's what changes people. When they see you sacrifice issues and realize love. Because we are children of God and we want people restored to our Father. **I stop trying to build and fix people specifically and started helping build/restore their relationship with the Father, and their character was built in**

that. I'd first help restore them to the Father not to the church or religion.

Religion and church are tools that we use on Earth to live right. We should live right (Romans 2:21) and go to church (Hebrews 10:25). But God wants for us to worship Him personally in spirit and truth (John 4:24). **Religion is never a good substitute for an intimate relationship with God.** Loving God is the focus and when you're thinking about looking, talking, and acting a certain way, you get side tracked and forget about Jesus and focus on acting like something and not "being" someone with true heart change. The Holy Spirit will convict other people. We are just the messengers. The Holy Spirit and God's Word will transform them (Romans 12:2). Generally, people know what they do wrong, because the Law of God is in our hearts (Jeremiah 31:33). When they fall in love with Jesus their hearts will become tender.

Then they will live for God and not only because the word states to but because they love Him and want to be with Him. When we *are* a witness, people will respond to *the heart of God in you*. When they see His love in you they will draw towards God (Romans 5:1/ John 4:8). If we make people focus on their sin and how wrong it is, rather than helping them become intimate with the Father, they become intimate with how bad sin is. Instead of turning from sin and being intimate with God and seeking Him, nit-picking their sin will keep them focused on it. We must remind everyone of God's goodness (Romans 2:4), His love, His grace, His mercy, His sacrifice, Jesus, the blood, and the covenant.

God doesn't want us to bask in the thought of how bad our sin is but to bask in His presence by loving on Him. We do this by focusing on God not ourselves. Know the state of people. Know their identity in Christ, and not so much about all their flaws. God's love shines brighter over all. Leading people to salvation through Jesus, then later if they solely lean on principles rather than Jesus it will get them lost again (Galatians 3:3). Fall in love and follow Jesus. Our service in the kingdom is to bring the family back together and mainly to the Father. **To be a witness by who we "are".** As a kingdom we have to work together, because many hands make the load light with the whole body of Christ working together. **Local bodies are not just the body of Christ, but all churches in the Kingdom make up the body.**

Conclusion

These things may really all intertwine from God's provision and the love of God for us. But here we now see an amazing picture of a generation hopeless, loved, and then made royalty. We can hold fast to it in our minds to ground us in our identity of our love relationship, of who we are, and of our inheritance. Royalty is not just a representation of our identity but also of our relationship — who we are connected to. We are God's precious children. It doesn't matter what year you live in or what generation, you are now a Royal Generation that was catalyzed by love.

Letter from Writer

Jesus is everything. In the end, this book will pass away. **I hope this book leads you towards God, not toward "self "improvement.** Sometimes it's easy to get lost in self-development instead of manifesting the image God already made us in. Our lives have to be all about loving God with all your heart and loving people! This has to be our passion, not the things of the world, the politics of the church, leadership principles, but pure passion for Jesus. The byproduct of this will bear all (Matthew 6:33).

Focus on Jesus and when you think you're focused, refocus to focus on Jesus (John 9:39).

> *[39] And Jesus said, "For judgment I have come into this world, that those who do not see may see, and that those who see may be made blind." (John 9:39 NKJV)*

My dream......

[16] Then those who feared the LORD spoke to one another,
And the LORD listened and heard them;
So a book of remembrance was written before Him
For those who fear the LORD
And who meditate on His name.

[17] "They shall be Mine," says the LORD of hosts,
"On the day that I make them My jewels.
And I will spare them As a man spares his own son who serves him.". (Malachi 3:16-17 NKJV)

When I was 17 years old, asleep at my mother's home, I had a dream. In my dream I woke up and Jesus was standing in my door way. He looked at me and asked, "Do you want to help me with my coming?"

I stared at Him speechless not knowing how to respond or the depth of what He was even asking. I mean I'm a kid and Jesus is standing over me!

Obviously He knew what I was thinking because He replied, "Think about it and I will come back tomorrow." He walked out of the room and shortly later in my dream being the next day Jesus walks back in. He asked "Did you think about it?"

I replied, "Yes" and agreed to help.

He said, "Remember Malachi," and disappeared from the room.

Then I actually woke up and told my Mother about the dream. I didn't even know what the word or name Malachi meant. She insisted it was in the Bible and I insisted that it wasn't. Neither of us was very religious. At that time, I didn't believe and neither did she. But, I gave my mother the benefit of the doubt and went to investigate. I found Malachi to be the last book of the Old Testament. I read it for ten years to try to comprehend what Jesus was communicating. For all ten years, from age 17 to age 27, I would read it and forget the last sentence soon as I read it. I would read the whole book periodically through the years and understood nothing. I would become very angry but I wouldn't lose hope because, I knew the dream was a real message to me and confirmed.

I looked up the Hebrew meaning of Malachi, the meaning is "my messenger or His Messenger". I really began to understand what He was communicating. In 2014, I read the book and my heart melted with words calling His people. I've read Malachi repeatedly. The verse that finally had me was Malachi 3:16-17. His people talked about the Father and honored Him, that He will be our God and we will be His own special treasure, we will be His *children*.

God is calling us back to His heart —to be our Father and us be His *children*. Not just in confession but in our *hearts*. He wants us to want to know His heart and to develop our everlasting relationship with Him. **The Gospel reveals the heart of the Father; Christian ideology reveals the ideas of humans.** The Gospel will always produce a more powerful fruit than Christian ideology. To seek Him with our hearts not our brain; to have intimate relationship rather than try to figure Him out. Seek His heart before His brain. He brings knowledge of the Kingdom as a byproduct of intimacy with His heart. Just seek Him for the person that He is within Himself. He is enough for us and we are quenched by Him alone. Be ecstatically in love with Him. Our identity is in His Heart. Seek relationship. Love the Father, He loves you.

www.ingramcontent.com/pod-product-compliance
Lightning Source LLC
Chambersburg PA
CBHW060645030426
42337CB00018B/3459